MANGA SHAKESPEARE™

1, -99

RICHARD III

ILLUSTRATED BY
PATRICK WARREN

Published by
SelfMadeHero
A division of Metro Media Ltd
5 Upper Wimpole Street
London W1G 6BP
www.selfmadehero.com

This edition published 2007

Illustrator: Patrick Warren
Text Adaptor: Richard Appignanesi
Designer: Andy Huckle
Textual Consultant: Nick de Somogyi
Publisher: Emma Hayley

ISBN-13: 978-0-9552856-3-9

10 9 8 7 6 5 4 3 2 1
Printed and bound in England

Medieval England. Two warring Houses –
Lancaster and York – vie for the English Crown.
No one was prepared for what would happen
next. It was to become one of the most brutal
episodes in England's history...

"I am determined to prove a villain."

Richard, Duke of Gloucester, later King Richard III

From the House of Lancaster

"Which of you trembles
not that looks on me?"

Queen Margaret, widow
of King Henry VI

Lady Anne Neville, widow
of Edward, Prince of Wales

"O, unpleasing news!"

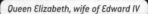
From the House of York

Queen Elizabeth, wife of Edward IV

"Ah me! I see the ruin of my house!"

The Duchess of York, mother of Richard, Edward, and Clarence

"Alas! I am the mother of these griefs."

King Edward IV, brother to Richard

"I entreat true peace of you…"

Richard's victims in the House of York

George, Duke of Clarence, brother to Richard

"I think there is no man secure..."

Clarence's children

"Is our father dead?"

King Edward's son, the Prince of Wales

"I fear no uncles dead..."

Other victims
King Edward's son, the Duke of York
"I shall not sleep in quiet at the Tower."
Lord Grey, son of Queen Elizabeth
"Now Margaret's curse has fallen upon our heads!"
Lord Rivers, brother of Queen Elizabeth
"In those days we followed our lawful King…"

... the Battle of Bosworth would herald a new dawn for the English monarchy.

"A horse! A horse! My kingdom for a horse!"

"God and Saint George! Richmond and victory!"

 Henry Richmond, later King Henry VII

WARS OF THE ROSES

THE RIVAL HOUSES OF LANCASTER (RED ROSE) AND YORK (WHITE ROSE) ARE BOTH DESCENDANTS OF THE PLANTAGENET ('BROOM FLOWER' IN FRENCH) LINE OF ENGLAND'S KINGS, ENDING WITH RICHARD II IN 1399.

THE STRUGGLES BETWEEN THESE TWO HOUSES TO GAIN POSSESSION OF THE ENGLISH CROWN ARE KNOWN AS THE WARS OF THE ROSES (1455-85). THIS IS A CHART OF THEIR FAMILY TREES WHICH SHOWS SOME OF THE MAIN CHARACTERS YOU WILL MEET IN *RICHARD III*.

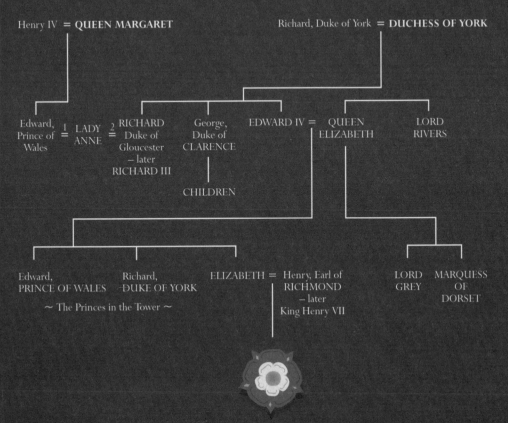

LANCASTER

YORK

Henry IV = **QUEEN MARGARET**

Richard, Duke of York = **DUCHESS OF YORK**

Edward, Prince of Wales $=_1$ LADY ANNE $_2=$ RICHARD Duke of Gloucester — later RICHARD III

George, Duke of CLARENCE

EDWARD IV = QUEEN ELIZABETH

LORD RIVERS

CHILDREN

Edward, PRINCE OF WALES

Richard, DUKE OF YORK

~ The Princes in the Tower ~

ELIZABETH = Henry, Earl of RICHMOND — later King Henry VII

LORD GREY

MARQUESS OF DORSET

TUDOR

EPISODES IN THE WARS OF THE ROSES

RICHARD, DUKE OF YORK, AND THE EARL OF WARWICK CHALLENGED THE LANCASTRIAN KING HENRY VI. RICHARD OF YORK WAS KILLED BUT HIS SON EDWARD IV SEIZED THE CROWN IN 1461. HENRY VI WAS BRIEFLY RESTORED IN 1470.

EDWARD IV REGAINED THE THRONE AT TEWKESBURY IN 1471. IN THIS BATTLE, EDWARD IV'S BROTHER RICHARD, DUKE OF GLOUCESTER (WHO BECAME KING RICHARD III IN 1483) KILLED HENRY VI'S SON EDWARD, PRINCE OF WALES, AND SOON AFTER MARRIED THE PRINCE'S WIDOW LADY ANNE NEVILLE. HENRY VI WAS IMPRISONED IN THE TOWER OF LONDON AND MURDERED THERE IN 1471.

NOW IS THE WINTER
OF OUR DISCONTENT
MADE GLORIOUS SUMMER
BY THIS SUN OF YORK.

NOW ARE
OUR BROWS
BOUND WITH
VICTORIOUS WREATHS...

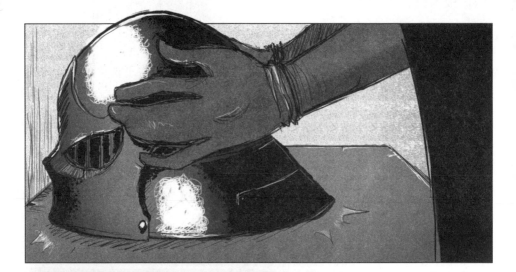

BUT I AM NOT SHAPED FOR AN
AMOROUS LOOKING-GLASS.
I AM RUDELY STAMPED,
DEFORMED, SO LAMELY THAT
DOGS BARK AT ME.

AND THEREFORE, SINCE I CANNOT PROVE A LOVER, I AM DETERMINED TO PROVE A VILLAIN, AND HATE THE IDLE PLEASURES OF THESE DAYS.

PLOTS HAVE I LAID TO SET MY BROTHER CLARENCE AND THE KING IN DEADLY HATE. A PROPHECY SAYS THAT "G" OF EDWARD'S HEIRS THE MURDERER SHALL BE.

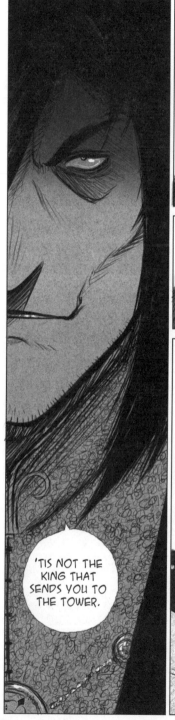

'TIS NOT THE KING THAT SENDS YOU TO THE TOWER.

HIS WIFE, CLARENCE, 'TIS SHE THAT TEMPERS HIM TO THIS EXTREMITY. WE ARE NOT SAFE, CLARENCE, WE ARE NOT SAFE.

WHAT NEWS
ABROAD?

THE KING IS
SICKLY, WEAK AND
MELANCHOLY.

WHAT,
IS HE IN
HIS BED?

HE IS.

HE CANNOT LIVE,
I HOPE, AND MUST
NOT DIE TILL GEORGE BE
PACKED WITH POST-HORSE
UP TO HEAVEN.

I'LL URGE HIS
HATRED MORE TO
CLARENCE...

IF I FAIL NOT IN MY
DEEP INTENT,
CLARENCE HATH NOT
ANOTHER DAY TO LIVE.
WHICH DONE, GOD
TAKE KING EDWARD TO
HIS MERCY —
AND LEAVE THE WORLD
FOR ME TO BUSTLE IN!

FOR THEN I'LL MARRY WARWICK'S YOUNGEST DAUGHTER.

WHAT THOUGH I KILLED HER HUSBAND AND HER FATHER?

THE READIEST WAY TO MAKE THE WENCH AMENDS IS TO BECOME HER HUSBAND AND HER FATHER.

UPON MY LIFE, SHE FINDS, ALTHOUGH I CANNOT, MYSELF TO BE A MARVELLOUS PROPER MAN.

WHOOMPH!

I'LL ENTERTAIN A SCORE OR TWO OF TAILORS TO STUDY FASHIONS TO ADORN MY BODY. SHINE OUT, FAIR SUN, TILL I HAVE BOUGHT A GLASS, THAT I MAY SEE MY SHADOW AS I PASS.

THEY DO ME WRONG, AND I WILL NOT ENDURE IT!

WHO ARE THEY THAT COMPLAIN UNTO THE KING AND FILL HIS EARS WITH SUCH DISSENTIOUS RUMOURS?

BECAUSE I CANNOT FLATTER AND SPEAK FAIR, I MUST BE HELD A RANCOROUS ENEMY.

48

HEAR ME, YOU WRANGLING PIRATES, THAT FALL OUT IN SHARING THAT WHICH YOU HAVE PILLAGED FROM ME!

WHICH OF YOU TREMBLES NOT THAT LOOKS ON ME?

I BEING QUEEN, BY YOU DEPOSED.

AH, GENTLE VILLAIN! DO NOT TURN AWAY.

FOUL WRINKLED WITCH, WERT THOU NOT BANISHED ON PAIN OF DEATH?

A HUSBAND
AND A SON THOU
OWEST TO ME.

AND ALL THE
PLEASURES YOU
USURP ARE MINE.

WHAT! WERE YOU SNARLING ALL BEFORE I CAME, READY TO CATCH EACH OTHER BY THE THROAT, AND TURN ALL YOUR HATRED NOW ON ME?

CAN CURSES PIERCE THE CLOUDS AND ENTER HEAVEN? WHY THEN, GIVE WAY, DULL CLOUDS, TO MY QUICK CURSES!

EDWARD, THY SON, DIE IN HIS YOUTH BY UNTIMELY VIOLENCE!
LONG MAYST THOU LIVE TO WAIL THY CHILDREN'S LOSS.

DIE NEITHER MOTHER NOR WIFE, NOR ENGLAND'S QUEEN!

RIVERS AND DORSET, YOU STANDERS-BY, AND THOU, LORD HASTINGS – GOD, I PRAY HIM, THAT NONE OF YOU MAY LIVE YOUR NATURAL AGE, BUT BY SOME UNLOOKED ACCIDENT CUT OFF.

HAVE DONE, THOU HATEFUL WITHERED HAG!

O BUCKINGHAM! TAKE HEED OF YONDER DOG. HIS VENOM TOOTH WILL RANKLE TO THE DEATH. BEWARE OF HIM. SIN, DEATH AND HELL HAVE SET THEIR MARKS ON HIM.

PEACE, PEACE! FOR SHAME, IF NOT FOR CHARITY.

MY HAIR DOTH STAND ON END TO HEAR HER CURSES.

THE SECRET MISCHIEFS THAT I SET ABROACH I LAY UNTO THE GRIEVOUS CHARGE OF OTHERS.

I SIGH, AND WITH A PIECE OF SCRIPTURE, TELL THEM THAT GOD BIDS US DO GOOD FOR EVIL.

AND THUS I CLOTHE MY NAKED VILLAINY WITH ODD OLD ENDS STOLEN FORTH OF HOLY WRIT, AND SEEM A SAINT WHEN MOST I PLAY THE DEVIL.

O, I HAVE PASSED A MISERABLE NIGHT, SO FULL OF GHASTLY DREAMS. I WOULD NOT SPEND ANOTHER THOUGH IT WERE TO BUY A WORLD OF HAPPY DAYS...

O GOD! EXECUTE THY WRATH ON ME ALONE. O, SPARE MY GUILTLESS WIFE AND MY POOR CHILDREN!

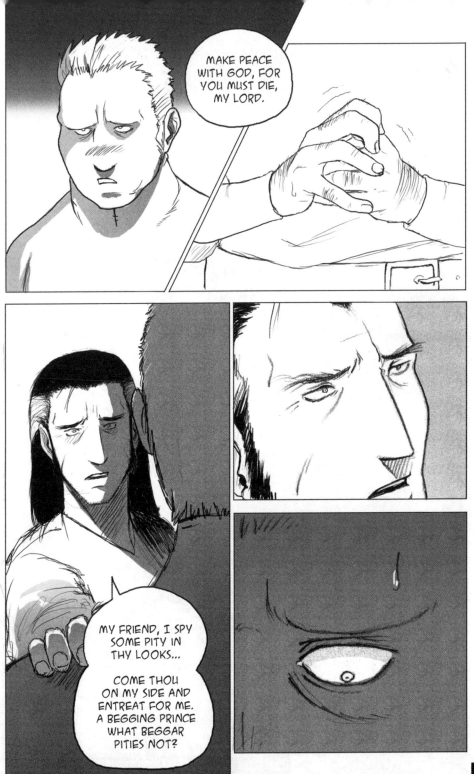

THE DYING KING EDWARD IV SEEKS TO ESTABLISH LASTING PEACE.

NOW HAVE I DONE A GOOD DAY'S WORK. MORE IN PEACE MY SOUL SHALL PART TO HEAVEN...

MADAM, SON DORSET, BUCKINGHAM — YOU HAVE BEEN FACTIOUS ONE AGAINST THE OTHER.

I WILL NEVER MORE REMEMBER OUR FORMER HATRED.

THIS INTERCHANGE OF LOVE UPON MY PART SHALL BE INVIOLABLE.

AND SO SWEAR I.

WHO SPOKE OF
BROTHERHOOD?
WHO SPOKE OF LOVE?
IN THE FIELD AT
TEWKESBURY, HE
RESCUED ME, AND SAID,
"DEAR BROTHER, LIVE,
AND BE A KING."

FROZEN ALMOST TO
DEATH, HE DID LAP
ME IN HIS GARMENTS.

THE PROUDEST OF YOU ALL HAVE BEEN BEHOLDING TO HIM.

YET NONE OF YOU WOULD ONCE BEG FOR HIS LIFE.

O GOD! I FEAR THY JUSTICE WILL TAKE HOLD ON ME AND YOU, AND MINE AND YOURS FOR THIS.

O! POOR CLARENCE!

MARKED YOU NOT HOW THE GUILTY KINDRED OF THE QUEEN LOOKED PALE WHEN THEY DID HEAR OF CLARENCE'S DEATH?

GOD WILL REVENGE IT.

SOMETIME LATER, A MESSENGER ARRIVES...

HOW DOTH THE PRINCE?

WELL, MADAM, AND IN HEALTH.

WHAT IS THY NEWS?

LORD RIVERS AND LORD GREY ARE SENT TO POMFRET, WITH THEM SIR THOMAS VAUGHAN — PRISONERS.

WHO HATH COMMITTED THEM?

GLOUCESTER AND BUCKINGHAM. WHY THE NOBLES WERE COMMITTED IS ALL UNKNOWN TO ME.

AH ME!
I SEE THE RUIN
OF MY HOUSE!

WELCOME, DESTRUCTION,
DEATH AND MASSACRE!
I SEE, AS IN A MAP,
THE END OF ALL.

ACCURSED AND UNQUIET
WRANGLING DAYS,
HOW MANY OF
YOU HAVE MINE
EYES BEHELD!

THE CONQUERORS MAKE
WAR UPON THEMSELVES,
BROTHER TO BROTHER,
BLOOD TO BLOOD,
SELF AGAINST SELF.

LET ME DIE TO LOOK
ON DEATH NO MORE.

PRINCE EDWARD, HEIR TO THE THRONE, COMES TO THE TOWER.

DEAR COUSIN, THE WEARY WAY HATH MADE YOU MELANCHOLY.

WELCOME, SWEET PRINCE, TO LONDON, TO YOUR CHAMBER.

NO, UNCLE, BUT I WANT MORE UNCLES HERE TO WELCOME ME.

THOSE UNCLES WHICH YOU WANT WERE DANGEROUS. YOUR GRACE ATTENDED TO THEIR SUGARED WORDS, BUT LOOKED NOT ON THE POISON OF THEIR HEARTS.

TELL ME WHAT THEY DESERVE THAT DO CONSPIRE MY DEATH WITH DEVILISH PLOTS OF DAMNED WITCHCRAFT?

I SAY, MY LORD, THEY HAVE DESERVED DEATH.

THEN LOOK HOW I AM BEWITCHED! BEHOLD, MINE ARM IS LIKE A BLASTED SAPLING WITHERED UP! AND THIS IS EDWARD'S WIFE THAT BY WITCHCRAFT THUS MARKED ME.

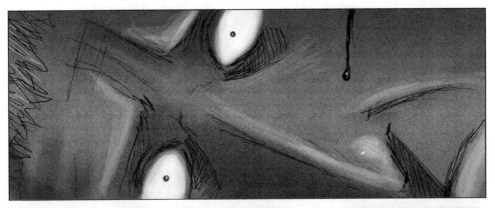

WOULD YOU BELIEVE THE SUBTLE TRAITOR THIS DAY HAD PLOTTED TO MURDER ME AND MY GOOD LORD OF GLOUCESTER?

HAD HE DONE SO?

HE DESERVED HIS DEATH, AND YOUR GOOD GRACES BOTH HAVE WELL PROCEEDED TO WARN FALSE TRAITORS FROM THE LIKE ATTEMPTS.

BUT I'LL ACQUAINT OUR DUTEOUS CITIZENS WITH ALL YOUR JUST PROCEEDINGS IN THIS CAUSE.

TELL THEM, WHEN MY MOTHER WENT WITH CHILD OF THAT INSATIATE EDWARD, MY PRINCELY FATHER THEN HAD WARS IN FRANCE... AND BY TRUE COMPUTATION OF THE TIME, FOUND THAT THE ISSUE WAS NOT HIS BEGOT.

YET TOUCH THIS SPARINGLY, BECAUSE, MY LORD, YOU KNOW MY MOTHER LIVES.

DOUBT NOT, MY LORD. I'LL PLAY THE ORATOR.

111

YOU SAY THAT EDWARD IS YOUR BROTHER'S SON? A DISTRESSED WIDOW MADE PRIZE OF HIS WANTON EYE, AND BY HER, IN HIS UNLAWFUL BED, HE GOT THIS EDWARD WHOM OUR MANNERS CALL THE PRINCE!

YET WHETHER YOU ACCEPT OUR SUIT OR NO, YOUR BROTHER'S SON SHALL NEVER REIGN OUR KING. WE WILL PLANT SOME OTHER IN THE THRONE, TO THE DISGRACE AND DOWNFALL OF YOUR HOUSE.

SINCE YOU WILL BUCKLE FORTUNE ON MY BACK TO BEAR HER BURDEN WHETHER I WILL. OR NO, I MUST HAVE PATIENCE TO ENDURE THE LOAD..

ENTER LORD STANLEY AND THE MARQUESS OF DORSET

LET ME SALUTE TWO FAIR QUEENS... COME, MADAM, YOU MUST STRAIGHT TO WESTMINSTER, THERE TO BE CROWNED RICHARD'S ROYAL QUEEN.

O, UNPLEASING NEWS!

O, DORSET! GO FROM THIS SLAUGHTER-HOUSE.

HA! AM I KING? BUT EDWARD LIVES.

HAVE I THY CONSENT THAT THEY SHALL DIE?

GIVE ME SOME LITTLE BREATH, DEAR LORD. I WILL RESOLVE YOU HEREIN PRESENTLY.

HIGH-REACHING BUCKINGHAM GROWS CIRCUMSPECT...

BUCKINGHAM SO LONG HELD OUT WITH ME UNTIRED, AND STOPS HE NOW FOR BREATH?

HOW NOW, LORD STANLEY! WHAT'S THE NEWS?

KNOW, MY LORD, THE MARQUESS DORSET IS FLED TO RICHMOND.

COME HITHER, CATESBY! RUMOUR IT ABROAD THAT ANNE MY QUEEN IS SICK AND LIKE TO DIE.

JAMES TYRRELL, YOUR MOST OBEDIENT SUBJECT.

ART THOU INDEED? TWO DEEP ENEMIES I WOULD HAVE THEE DEAL UPON. I MEAN THOSE BASTARDS IN THE TOWER.

I'LL RID YOU FROM THE FEAR OF THEM.

SAY IT IS DONE AND I WILL LOVE THEE AND PREFER THEE FOR IT.

THE SONS OF EDWARD SLEEP AND ANNE MY WIFE HATH BID THE WORLD GOOD NIGHT.

NOW, FOR I KNOW RICHMOND AIMS AT YOUNG ELIZABETH, MY BROTHER'S DAUGHTER, AND BY THAT KNOT LOOKS PROUDLY ON THE CROWN...

TO HER GO I, A JOLLY THRIVING WOOER.

QUEEN MARGARET WITH THE DUCHESS OF YORK AND QUEEN ELIZABETH.

FROM FORTH THE KENNEL OF THY WOMB HATH CREPT A HELL-HOUND THAT DOTH HUNT US ALL TO DEATH.

O, HARRY'S WIFE, TRIUMPH NOT IN MY WOES. GOD WITNESS WITH ME, I HAVE WEPT FOR THINE.

I AM HUNGRY FOR REVENGE, AND NOW I CLOY ME WITH BEHOLDING IT. RICHARD YET LIVES, HELL'S BLACK INTELLIGENCER. DEAR GOD! I PRAY THAT I MAY LIVE TO SAY, "THE DOG IS DEAD."

139

143

AND SO FAREWELL, RELENTING FOOL AND SHALLOW CHANGING WOMAN!

LORD STANLEY, EARL OF DERBY BRINGS NEWS.

STANLEY, WHAT NEWS WITH YOU?

NONE GOOD, MY LIEGE. RICHMOND IS ON THE SEAS... STIRRED UP BY DORSET, BUCKINGHAM AND MORTON, HE MAKES FOR ENGLAND, HERE TO CLAIM THE CROWN.

147

SIX OR SEVEN THOUSAND IS THEIR UTMOST POWER.

WHY, OUR BATTALIA TREBLES THAT ACCOUNT. BESIDES, THE KING'S NAME IS A TOWER OF STRENGTH.

LET US SURVEY THE VANTAGE OF THE GROUND. CALL FOR SOME MEN OF SOUND DIRECTION. LET'S LACK NO DISCIPLINE, MAKE NO DELAY, FOR, LORDS, TOMORROW IS A BUSY DAY.

INTO MY TENT.
THE AIR IS RAW AND COLD.

COME, GENTLEMEN, LET US CONSULT UPON TOMORROW'S BUSINESS.

SEND OUT TO STANLEY'S REGIMENT. BID HIM BRING HIS POWER BEFORE SUN-RISING, LEST HIS SON GEORGE FALL INTO THE BLIND CAVE OF ETERNAL NIGHT.

SADDLE FOR THE FIELD TOMORROW. LOOK THAT MY STAVES BE SOUND AND NOT TOO HEAVY.

STANLEY VISITS RICHMOND IN HIS TENT.

FORTUNE AND VICTORY SIT ON THY HELM!

ALL COMFORT BE TO THY PERSON!

I, AS I MAY, WITH BEST ADVANTAGE WILL AID THEE IN THIS DOUBTFUL SHOCK OF ARMS. BUT I MAY NOT BE TOO FORWARD, LEST TENDER GEORGE BE EXECUTED IN HIS FATHER'S SIGHT.

ADIEU. BE VALIANT AND SPEED WELL!

I'LL STRIVE, WITH TROUBLED THOUGHTS, TO TAKE A NAP..

O THOU, WHOSE CAPTAIN I ACCOUNT MYSELF, LOOK ON MY FORCES WITH A GRACIOUS EYE. TO THEE I DO COMMEND MY WATCHFUL SOUL, ERE I LET FALL THE WINDOWS OF MINE EYES.

SLEEPING AND WAKING, O DEFEND ME STILL!

LET ME SIT HEAVY ON THY SOUL TOMORROW!

THE GHOSTS OF RICHARD'S VICTIMS APPEAR IN DREAMS TO HIM AND RICHMOND.

THINK HOW THOU STABB'ST ME IN MY PRIME OF YOUTH AT TEWKESBURY. DESPAIR, THEREFORE, AND DIE!

BE CHEERFUL, RICHMOND, FOR THE WRONGED SOULS OF BUTCHERED PRINCES FIGHT IN THY BEHALF.

KING HENRY'S ISSUE, RICHMOND, COMFORTS THEE.

WHEN I WAS MORTAL,
MY ANOINTED BODY
BY THEE WAS PUNCHED
FULL OF DEADLY
HOLES. THINK ON
THE TOWER AND ME.
DESPAIR AND DIE!

HENRY THE SIXTH BIDS
THEE DESPAIR AND DIE.

VIRTUOUS AND HOLY,
BE THOU CONQUEROR!

HARRY, THAT
PROPHESIED THOU
SHOULDST BE
THE KING, DOTH
COMFORT THEE IN
THY SLEEP. LIVE THOU
AND FLOURISH!

THOU OFFSPRING OF THE HOUSE OF LANCASTER, THE WRONGED HEIRS OF YORK DO PRAY FOR THEE. GOOD ANGELS GUARD THY BATTLE! LIVE AND FLOURISH!

THE GHOSTS OF RIVERS, GREY AND VAUGHAN...
LET ME SIT HEAVY ON THY SOUL TOMORROW! RIVERS THAT DIED AT POMFRET! DESPAIR AND DIE!
THINK UPON GREY AND LET THY SOUL DESPAIR.
THINK UPON VAUGHAN, AND WITH GUILTY FEAR, DESPAIR AND DIE!

AWAKE!
AND THINK
OUR WRONGS IN
RICHARD'S BOSOM
WILL CONQUER HIM.

AWAKE, AND
WIN THE DAY!

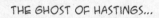
THE GHOST OF HASTINGS...

BLOODY AND GUILTY,
GUILTILY AWAKE,
AND IN A BLOODY BATTLE
END THY DAYS!
THINK ON LORD HASTINGS,
DESPAIR AND DIE!

QUIET, UNTROUBLED SOUL, AWAKE, AWAKE! ARM, FIGHT AND CONQUER FOR FAIR ENGLAND'S SAKE!

THE GHOSTS OF THE TWO
YOUNG PRINCES...

DREAM ON THY COUSINS,
SMOTHERED IN
THE TOWER.
LET US BE LEAD WITHIN
THY BOSOM, RICHARD,
AND WEIGH THEE
DOWN TO RUIN,
SHAME AND DEATH!

THY NEPHEWS' SOULS
BID THEE DESPAIR
AND DIE!

SLEEP, RICHMOND, SLEEP IN PEACE, AND WAKE IN JOY. GOOD ANGELS GUARD THEE FROM THE BOAR'S ANNOY!

LIVE AND BEGET A HAPPY RACE OF KINGS! EDWARD'S UNHAPPY SONS DO BID THEE FLOURISH.

THE GHOST OF LADY ANNE...
RICHARD, THY WIFE, WRETCHED ANNE THAT NEVER SLEPT A QUIET HOUR WITH THEE, NOW FILLS THY SLEEP WITH PERTURBATIONS.
TOMORROW IN THE BATTLE THINK ON ME. DESPAIR AND DIE!

THE FIRST WAS I THAT HELPED
THEE TO THE CROWN.
THE LAST WAS I THAT
FELT THY TYRANNY.
O, IN THE BATTLE THINK ON
BUCKINGHAM AND DIE IN
TERROR OF THY GUILTINESS!

DREAM ON OF BLOODY
DEEDS AND DEATH.
DESPAIRING,
YIELD THY BREATH!

I DIED FOR HOPE ERE I COULD LEND THEE AID.

BUT CHEER THY HEART AND BE THOU NOT DISMAYED. GOD AND GOOD ANGELS FIGHT ON RICHMOND'S SIDE.

AND RICHARD FALLS IN HEIGHT OF ALL HIS PRIDE.

183

BY THE APOSTLE PAUL, SHADOWS TONIGHT HAVE STRUCK MORE TERROR TO THE SOUL OF RICHARD THAN CAN THE SUBSTANCE OF TEN THOUSAND SOLDIERS LED BY SHALLOW RICHMOND.

COME, GO WITH ME. UNDER OUR TENTS I'LL PLAY THE EAVESDROPPER TO HEAR IF ANY MEAN TO SHRINK FROM ME.

GOD AND OUR GOOD CAUSE FIGHT UPON OUR SIDE. THOSE WHOM WE FIGHT AGAINST HAD RATHER HAVE US WIN THAN HIM THEY FOLLOW. FOR WHAT IS HE THEY FOLLOW? TRULY, GENTLEMEN, A BLOODY TYRANT AND A HOMICIDE.

THEN, IN THE NAME OF GOD, ADVANCE YOUR STANDARDS, DRAW YOUR WILLING SWORDS! SOUND DRUMS AND TRUMPETS, BOLDLY AND CHEERFULLY. GOD AND SAINT GEORGE! RICHMOND AND VICTORY!

WHO SAW THE SUN TODAY?

NOT I, MY LORD.

A BLACK DAY WILL IT BE TO SOMEBODY. WHY, WHAT IS THAT TO ME MORE THAN TO RICHMOND? FOR THE SELF-SAME HEAVEN THAT FROWNS ON ME LOOKS SADLY UPON HIM.

REMEMBER WHOM YOU ARE TO COPE WITHAL. A SORT OF VAGABONDS, RASCALS AND RUN-AWAYS...

AND WHO DOTH LEAD THEM BUT A PALTRY FELLOW.

LET'S WHIP THESE STRAGGLERS OVER THE SEA AGAIN. THESE FAMISHED BEGGARS, WEARY OF THEIR LIVES...

A THOUSAND HEARTS ARE GREAT WITHIN MY BOSOM.

ADVANCE OUR STANDARDS! SET UPON OUR FOES! OUR ANCIENT WORD OF COURAGE, FAIR SAINT GEORGE, INSPIRE US WITH THE SPLEEN OF FIERY DRAGONS!

UPON THEM! VICTORY SITS UPON OUR HELMS.

CATESBY SEEKS HELP ON THE BATTLEFIELD.

RESCUE, MY LORD OF NORFOLK! RESCUE!

THE KING ENACTS MORE WONDERS THAN A MAN, DARING AN OPPOSITE TO EVERY DANGER.

INTER THEIR
BODIES AS
BECOMES
THEIR
BIRTHS.

PROCLAIM A PARDON
TO THE SOLDIERS
FLED THAT IN
SUBMISSION WILL
RETURN TO US.
WE WILL UNITE
THE WHITE ROSE
AND THE RED.

SMILE, HEAVEN, UPON
THIS FAIR
CONJUNCTION.

ENGLAND HATH LONG BEEN
MAD AND SCARRED HERSELF.

THE BROTHER BLINDLY SHED
THE BROTHER'S BLOOD,
THE FATHER RASHLY
SLAUGHTERED HIS
OWN SON, THE SON BEEN
BUTCHER TO THE SIRE.

ALL THIS DIVIDED YORK
AND LANCASTER —

AND LET THEIR HEIRS
ENRICH THE TIME TO
COME WITH PEACE,
SMILING PLENTY AND
FAIR PROSPEROUS
DAYS!
NOW CIVIL WOUNDS
ARE STOPPED,
PEACE LIVES AGAIN.
THAT SHE MAY
LONG LIVE HERE,
GOD SAY AMEN!

PLOT SUMMARY OF RICHARD III

The progress of Richard, Duke of Gloucester, to the English throne went on for twelve years. It began in 1471 with his killing of Edward, Prince of Wales, on the battlefield, the murder of King Henry VI in the Tower of London, and the rule of Richard's elder brother Edward IV until 1483 when at last he became King Richard III from 1483 to 1485. Shakespeare's story compresses those years into what seems a few months.

Richard III is set against the background of the long civil war known as the Wars of the Roses, between the royal families of York (of which he is a member) and of Lancaster (overthrown at the defeat and death of Henry VI). Richard, a physically deformed, ambitious villain, aspires to become king and plots from the start to murder anyone, including his own York kin who stand in his way. He seduces Lady Anne, widow of Henry VI's son, Edward, marries her, and later kills her when she has served her purpose. He executes his own brother Clarence in the Tower, shifts the blame on to the sickly Edward IV to hasten his death, and becomes Lord Protector of England.

Queen Margaret, widow of Henry VI, curses him and warns the court of his evil plotting, but he proceeds to kill the noblemen loyal to Edward IV's heirs – the kinsmen of Edward's wife, Queen Elizabeth – and hires murderers to dispose of the young princes he has imprisoned in the Tower. With the aid of Lord Buckingham – also later executed – Richard is crowned King of England. Richard now seeks to marry his own niece, young Elizabeth, daughter of Queen Elizabeth and Edward IV, to secure his power base.

Henry Tudor, Earl of Richmond, a descendant of the Lancasters, is meanwhile gathering forces of opposition to counter Richard. On the night before the final battle, the ghosts of all those murdered by Richard appear in a dream, promising defeat for him and victory to Richmond. Richard is slain at the Battle of Bosworth. Richmond is crowned as King Henry VII, marries Princess Elizabeth, and thereby unites the red rose of Lancaster with the white rose of York – and so begins the era of the Tudor dynasty in which Shakespeare himself lived.

A BRIEF LIFE OF WILLIAM SHAKESPEARE

Shakespeare's birthday is traditionally said to be the 23rd of April – St George's Day, patron saint of England. A good start for England's greatest writer. But that date and even his name are uncertain. He signed his own name in different ways. "Shakespeare" is now the accepted one out of dozens of different versions.

He was born at Stratford-upon-Avon in 1564, and baptized on 26th April. His mother, Mary Arden, was the daughter of a prosperous farmer. His father John Shakespeare, a glove-maker, was a respected civic figure – and probably also a Catholic. In 1570, just as Will began school, his father was accused of illegal dealings. The family fell into debt and disrepute.

Will attended a local school for eight years. He did not go to university. The next ten years are a blank filled by suppositions. Was he briefly a Latin teacher, a soldier, a sea-faring explorer? Was he prosecuted and whipped for poaching deer?

We do know that in 1582 he married Anne Hathaway, eight years his senior, and three months pregnant. Two more children – twins – were born three years later but, by around 1590, Will had left Stratford to pursue a theatre career in London. Shakespeare's apprenticeship began as an actor and "pen for hire".

He learned his craft the hard way. He soon won fame as a playwright with often-staged popular hits.

He and his colleagues formed a stage company, the Lord Chamberlain's Men, which built the famous Globe Theatre. It opened in 1599 but was destroyed by fire in 1613 during a performance of *Henry VIII* which used gunpowder special effects. It was rebuilt in brick the following year.

Shakespeare was a financially successful writer who invested his money wisely in property. In 1597, he bought an enormous house in Stratford, and in 1608 became a shareholder in London's Blackfriars Theatre. He also redeemed the family's honour by acquiring a personal coat of arms.

Shakespeare wrote over 40 works, including poems, "lost" plays and collaborations, in a career spanning nearly 25 years. He retired to Stratford in 1613, where he died on 23rd April 1616, aged 52, apparently of a fever after a "merry meeting" of drinks with friends. Shakespeare did in fact die on St George's Day! He was buried "full 17 foot deep" in Holy Trinity Church, Stratford, and left an epitaph cursing anyone who dared disturb his bones.

There have been preposterous theories disputing Shakespeare's authorship. Some claim that Sir Francis Bacon (1561–1626), philosopher and Lord Chancellor, was the real author of Shakespeare's plays. Others propose Edward de Vere, Earl of Oxford (1550–1604), or, even more weirdly, Queen Elizabeth I. The implication is that the "real" Shakespeare had to be a university graduate or an aristocrat. Nothing less would do for the world's greatest writer.

Shakespeare is mysteriously hidden behind his work. His life will not tell us what inspired his genius.

MANGA SHAKESPEARE ™

EDITORIAL

Richard Appignanesi: Series Editor

Richard Appignanesi was a founder and co-director of the Writers & Readers Publishing Cooperative and Icon Books where he originated the internationally acclaimed Introducing series. His own best-selling titles written for the series include *Freud*, *Postmodernism* and *Existentialism*. He is also the author of the fiction trilogy *Italia Perversa* and the novel *Yukio Mishima's Report to the Emperor*. He is currently associate editor of the art and culture journal *Third Text* and reviews editor of the journal *Futures*. His latest book *What do Existentialists Believe?* was released in 2006.

Nick de Somogyi: Textual Consultant

Nick de Somogyi works as a freelance writer and researcher, as a genealogist at the College of Arms, and as a contributing editor to *New Theatre Quarterly*. He is the founding editor of the Globe Quartos series, and was the visiting curator at Shakespeare's Globe, 2003–6. His publications include *Shakespeare's Theatre of War* (1998), *Jokermen and Thieves: Bob Dylan and the Ballad Tradition* (1986), and, as editor, *The Little Book of War Poems* (1999), and (from 2001) the *Shakespeare Folios* series for Nick Hern Books. His other work has included contributions to the Open University (1995) and Carlton Television (2000), BBC Radio 3 and Radio 4, and the National Portrait Gallery (2006).

ARTIST

Patrick Warren

Patrick Warren is from Hammersmith in London and is currently studying Animation at the University of Westminster. He was a winner of Tokyopop's first UK Rising Stars of Manga competition in 2006. His interest in Japan began when he was eight and he had started doodling manga by the time he was 15. Patrick's influences include manga artists such as Hiroaki Samura, Tite Kubo, Oh! Great and Western artists such as Frank Miller and his own father. *Richard III* is Patrick's first full-length illustration work.

PUBLISHER

SelfMadeHero publishes manga and graphic novels. It launched its first titles in the Manga Shakespeare series with *Hamlet* and *Romeo and Juliet*. Other titles already published include: *The Tempest* and *A Midsummer Night's Dream*, with more to follow.

HAMLET

ROMEO AND JULIET

THE TEMPEST

A MIDSUMMER NIGHT'S DREAM

SELF MADE HERO

www.selfmadehero.com